Freedom From Fat
CHINESE HOME COOKING

Chinese Traditional Meals

by Ting Gee

Benting & Company, Tucson, 1997

Published by Benting & Company

Printed in the United States of America

Library of Congress Catalog Card Number: 97-077820

Gee, Ting
Freedom From Fat Chinese Home Cooking
127 p.

ISBN 0-9661914-4-7

Dedication

For my parents, with love, who taught me
all about Chinese cuisine.

Contents

Sincere Thanks

I want to express my gratitude to my son Benji for being so patient and loving during this endeavor.

This book was inspired by a special friend, Frank Kalil, who is a master himself in "fat free" cuisine.

Thanks to Kate Taylor, Charlotte Tilson, Sinclair Browning, Alex Karahalios, and West•Press for providing invaluable help in the production of the book.

Photography by Don Winston and Erik Hinote

Recipe analysis by Linda Hutchings, M.A., R.D.

Introduction

My earliest memories all seem to involve the kitchen and our family cook, Ah-Zhen, at our home in Shanghai. Glorious smells and sizzling buns were often beckoning me and my little sister, Yin. The mere thought of her egg rolls makes my mouth water even today. Ah-Zhen was with our family for 30 years and was a kind and thoughtful teacher.

I moved to America when I was 21 and later married a physician. He taught me about healthy diets and the damage that high fat consumption had done to many of his patients. He loved my cooking and was always asking for more. It was time to rethink the recipes of dear Ah-Zhen.

Could a dish be steamed instead of fried? Was there a way to cut the fat in stir-fry dishes without affecting the taste? Did the oil, in fact, actually mask some delicious flavors? Was it possible to substitute chicken breast for pork or beef? After several years of experiments, I found that my favorite dishes could be modified without loss of flavor. Most of the recipes, our enthusiastic friends, patients and guests assured me, tasted even better. They all urged me to write them down and share them with everyone.

I learned Americans love tasty meals. Chinese food is ever growing in popularity. Here are the dishes I have found where reducing the fat actually enhances the taste. This allows you and your loved ones to seriously limit fat intake and still satisfy your craving for delicious, balanced Chinese meals.

I hope you will enjoy these dishes and you too will discover that low fat meals can be delicious, balanced and bursting with flavor.

If you have any questions or comments, feel free to contact me at the address below. Please visit my web site for bonus recipes and upcoming publications

Eat well and enjoy in good health!

Ting Gee
P.O. Box 65126, Tucson, AZ 85728
Ting@BenTing.com
http://www.BenTing.com

Ting Gee

Appetizers

Chinese Pancakes

*T*his is served with moo shu vegetables or moo shu chicken or any other dish you prefer to roll with and serve. They are also great to serve with soups.

Ingredients:
1 cup all purpose flour
1/2 cup boiling water
1 light vegetable oil spray

Directions:
Place flour in a large bowl. Add boiling water and mix well. Knead the dough on a floured board for 5 minutes. Roll the dough into a long roll. Cut the dough into 8 even segments. Roll each segment into a ball with the palms of your hands, then flatten them on the floured board. Spray one side of each pancake with light vegetable oil, then lay two on top of each other, sandwich style, making four stacks of pancakes. Roll each pancake stack into a 6 inch circle. Heat a nonstick pan on medium heat. Cook the pancakes on both sides until they puff up. Remove them from the pan and separate them into two pancakes.

When serving, put the filling on the smooth side of the pancake, then roll them with the rough side out.

To freeze, stack cool pancakes and place them in a plastic freezer bag. Steam for 10 minutes before serving.

Makes 8 pancakes

Calories per pancake: 58
Fat per pancake: 0.3 gram
Calories from fat: 5%

Pot Stickers

While waiting to ring in the New Year, my grandmother used to prepare truckloads of pot stickers for family and friends. You may choose hot sauce or mixed sauce for dipping. Serving pot stickers alone can be a whole meal or as an appetizer. Serve 4 to 6 pot stickers per person as an appetizer, or 15 to 20 per person as a meal.

Ingredients:

For the Filling:

1/4 lb. ground turkey breast
1 (10 oz.) package chopped frozen spinach,
   squeezed and drained
2 egg whites
1/4 cup chopped water chestnuts*
1/4 cup chopped Chinese pickles (optional)**
1 teaspoon minced fresh ginger
2 green onions, chopped
1 tablespoon rice wine or dry sherry
2 tablespoons oyster sauce**(can substitute soy sauce)
dash of salt
1/4 teaspoon garlic powder
dash of white pepper
2 (10 or 12 oz.) packages pot sticker or dumpling skins**
1/4 cup hot sauce (for serving)

For the Dipping Sauce:

1/4 cup soy sauce
1/4 cup vinegar
2 tablespoons sugar

*available at Asian markets and some supermarkets
**available at Asian markets

Preparation:

Mix ground turkey, spinach, egg whites, water chestnuts, ginger, green onions, rice wine, oyster sauce, salt, garlic powder and pepper together and allow to sit for 30 minutes before wrapping. Pour 1/2 cup of cold water in a small bowl for wrapping. Mix soy sauce, vinegar and sugar together, heat till sugar is dissolved. Set aside for serving.

To Wrap:

Put 1 tablespoon of mixture in middle of a pot sticker skin. Wet edges of skins with water so skin will stick together. Fold in half and pinch edges together.

To Cook:

In a large saucepan, fill half full with water and bring to a boil on high heat. Cook 25 pot stickers at one time. Stir them slowly while cooking so they do not stick together. Return to boil, add 1 cup of cold water. Cook and stir until water boils again, repeat the process until pot stickers are floating at the water level. Serve hot or cold with hot sauce or prepared sauce.

To Freeze:

Place uncooked pot stickers on a cookie sheet (make sure it fits in your freezer) with spaces in between. Leave in freezer for 30 minutes. Replace individual frozen pot stickers in plastic freezer bags. They will keep in freezer for one month. Cook in water as above.

Makes 60 pot stickers

Serving size: 5 pot stickers
Calories per serving: 40
Fat per serving: 0.47 gram
Calories from fat: 11%

Steamed Buns

The Southern Chinese consume rice as their main diet; the Northern Chinese consume flour, wheat and rice as their main diets. This is a basic bun recipe which can have different fillings such as sweet bean paste for breakfast, dim-sum, or chicken and vegetable fillings for breakfast and dim-sum. It also can be frozen and steamed again before serving.

Ingredients:
1 (1/4 oz.) package dry yeast
1 cup warm water
4 1/4 cups all purpose flour
1/4 cup sugar
1/2 cup hot water

Preparation:
Preheat oven to warm for 2 minutes, then turn off.

Directions:
In a large bowl, mix yeast and 1 cup of warm water until yeast is dissolved. Add 1 cup flour and mix well. Cover the bowl with a wet towel and let rise for 15 minutes.

In a small bowl, mix sugar and 1/2 cup hot water. Let cool, add to the mixture in the large bowl. Mix well. Add 3 1/2 cups of flour; mix thoroughly.

On a floured board, knead the dough for 5 minutes. Place the dough back in the large bowl, covering it again with the wet towel, then place the bowl in the warm (not hot!) oven. Allow the dough to rise for 2 hours.

Knead the dough for another 10 minutes, make a long roll 2 inches in diameter. Cut the long roll into 28 small segments and place each segment on a 2 x 3 inch sheet of waxed paper.

Place 7 rolls on each steam rack, leaving space between each bun, then let rise again for 10 minutes, then steam for 10 minutes. You can use a bamboo steamer as long as the pan fits into the steamer and it is possible to cover. Repeat again with the remaining buns.

Makes 28 buns

Calories per bun: 77
Fat per bun: 0.2 gram
Calories from fat: 3%

Stuffed Mushrooms

*T*his dish can be served as a side dish as well as an appetizer with a lettuce garnish. You can use shrimp substitute ground turkey, or, for a vegetarian version, substitute scrambled egg whites.

Ingredients:
20 large fresh mushrooms (prefer Golden Italian)

For the Filling:
1/2 lb. fresh shrimp, shelled, deveined, chopped
1 teaspoon minced ginger
3 cloves garlic, minced
1/4 cup chopped water chestnuts
2 green onions, chopped
1 tablespoon rice wine or dry sherry
1 tablespoon cornstarch
dash of salt
1 light vegetable oil spray

For the Sauce:
2 tablespoons oyster sauce*
3/4 cup vegetable stock or water
4 teaspoons cornstarch

20 cilantro leaves

available at Asian markets

Preparation:

Clean and break off stems of mushrooms. Mix shrimp, ginger, garlic, water chestnuts, green onions, rice wine, cornstarch and salt together. Stuff each mushroom with mixture, prepare the sauce.

Directions:

In a nonstick pan, spray one time with light vegetable oil and cook mushrooms with mixture side down and cook over medium high heat for 2 minutes. Turn them over and brown the other side. Repeat the rest. Place all mushrooms in pan with mixture side up, add sauce and cook for 1 minute. Serve with one cilantro leaf on each mushroom.

Makes 20 stuffed mushrooms

Calories per serving: 18
Fat per serving: 0.07 gram
Calories from fat: 4%

Sweet and Sour Sauce

Here is a fat-free version of an essential Chinese sauce which accompanies many wonderful dishes and appetizers.

Ingredients:
1/2 cup water
1/2 cup brown sugar
1/4 cup vinegar (rice or white)
1/2 cup ketchup
1 tablespoon cornstarch dissolved in 1/4 cup water

Directions:
In a small saucepan, heat water until it boils, then add sugar. Reduce heat to medium, add vinegar, ketchup and stir until ketchup is completely dissolved. Add dissolved cornstarch and stir until thick.

Makes 1 cup of sweet & sour sauce

Calories per tablespoon: 28
Fat per tablespoon: 0 grams
Calories from fat: 0%

"Un-Fried" Crab Cakes

Crab cakes are a great appetizer for adults and children.

Ingredients:
1 8 oz. fat free cream cheese
1 1/2 cups imitation crab
1 16 oz. package Won Ton skins*
1 light vegetable oil spray

available at Asian markets and some supermarkets

Preparation:
Preheat oven to 400. Break the crab meat apart and mix with fat free cream cheese in a medium bowl. Wrap mixture in the center of won ton skin after wetting two sides with water (along dotted lines).

Directions:
Spray a cookie sheet with light vegetable oil. Place crab cakes on prepared cookie sheet; leave 1/2 inch between cakes. Lightly spray each crab cake with light vegetable oil. Place cookie sheet on bottom shelf and bake for 5 minutes. Turn crab cakes over and bake another 3 minutes or until they are lightly browned and crispy on both sides. Serve hot with sweet and sour sauce (see page 11.)

Makes about 30 crab cakes

Calories per serving: 61
Fat per serving: 0.3 gram
Calories from fat: 5%

"Un-Fried" Egg Rolls

e gg rolls are served during the New Year to signify prosperity. However, because this dish is so well-loved, you may be serving it more often. Baking instead of frying makes this dish both guilt free and fat free. You may substitute julienned chicken breast or julienned baked tofu for the egg substitute in the filling if you prefer.

Ingredients:

10 dried black mushrooms*
1 egg white
1 light vegetable oil spray
4 oz. egg substitute
1 medium carrot, julienned
2 tablespoons water
3 cups julienned cabbage
1 cup bean sprouts
2 tablespoons oyster sauce*
dash of white pepper

1 teaspoon cornstarch dissolved in 2 tablespoons water

12 paper-thin egg roll wrappers*

*available at Asian markets and some supermarkets

Preparation:

Soak black mushrooms in hot water for 20 minutes, rinse, cut ends off, squeeze out excess water and julienne. Lightly beat the egg white to seal the egg rolls. Spray a cookie sheet with 3 sprays of light vegetable oil. Set aside. Preheat oven to 400˚.

Directions:

In a nonstick pan, scramble egg substitute with 1 spray of light vegetable oil until eggs are firm, use spatula to break them apart. Set aside.

In the same pan, cook shredded carrot in 2 tablespoons of water on high heat for 30 seconds; add mushrooms, shredded cabbage and cook for 1 minute, add bean sprouts and cook for 30 seconds. Add cooked egg to vegetables. Add oyster sauce, pepper and dissolved cornstarch. Set aside until cool.

To Wrap:

Place filling in bottom third of egg roll wrapper and bring the bottom point of the wrapper over the filling. Roll tightly and bring both right and left sides of the wrapper over. Dab the top point wrapper with water and roll it over snugly to seal and shut.

To Bake:

Place egg rolls evenly on the prepared cookie sheet. Lightly spray each egg roll with light vegetable oil. Place cookie sheet on the bottom shelf and bake for 15 minutes. Turn egg rolls over every 5 minutes until they are lightly brown and crispy on both sides. Serve hot with sweet and sour sauce.
(See page 11).

Makes 12 egg rolls

Calories per serving: 48
Fat per serving: 0.6 gram
Calories from fat: 12%

Soups

Chicken Stock

Homemade chicken stock is richer than canned chicken stock. You can use either one for recipes indicated in this book. However, be sure to skim fat from the stock before use. Stock can be frozen 1 month for later use.

Ingredients:

1 whole skinless chicken (about 3 lbs.)
8 cups water
3 green onions
6 slices fresh ginger root
1/4 cup rice wine or dry sherry
dash of salt

Directions:

Place chicken in a large pot. Add water (10 cups should be enough to cover the chicken); bring to a boil, then skim the foam off the top. Reduce heat, add green onions, ginger and wine. Simmer for 3 hours, add salt. Remove chicken, green onions and ginger (use a strainer if necessary) from the stock and place stock in refrigerator. When chilled, remove the layer of fat from the stock.

Makes 6 cups of stock

Calories per cup: 27
Fat per cup: 0.02 gram
Calories from fat: 7%

Cream of Corn Soup

A simple, fast and delicious soup to serve before main dishes.

Ingredients:

2 egg whites
1 cup stock (chicken or vegetable)
1 (15-oz.) can cream-style corn

Preparation:

Lightly beat the egg whites.

Directions:

Pour stock into a medium saucepan, add cream-style corn. Stir constantly over medium heat until the soup comes to a boil. Turn the heat off. In a counterclockwise direction, using chopsticks, slowly stir egg whites into the soup and stir for 15 seconds.

Serves 4

Calories per serving with chicken stock: 92
Fat per serving with chicken stock: 0.6 gram
Calories from fat: 6%

Calories per serving with vegetable stock: 87
Fat per serving with vegetable stock: 0.1 gram
Calories from fat: 4%

Egg Drop Soup

My grandmother used to serve egg drop soup with fried rice and I have loved it ever since I was a child.

Ingredients:
4 egg whites
4 cups stock (chicken or vegetable)
dash of salt
pinch of white pepper
1 green onion, chopped

Preparation:
Lightly beat the egg whites, set aside.

Directions:
In a medium saucepan, bring stock to a boil. Turn the heat off and slowly pour the egg whites into the stock, stirring clockwise for 20 seconds with chopsticks. Add salt, pepper and green onion to serve.

Serves 4

Calories per serving with chicken stock: 43
Fat per serving with chicken stock: 0.2 gram
Calories from fat: 5%

Calories per serving with vegetable stock: 27
Fat per serving with vegetable stock: trace
Calories from fat: 0%

Hot and Sour Soup

This soup is ripe with the wonderful flavors of Northern China. It can be served as a main dish along with Chinese pancakes or buns. Cook without golden lilies and wood ears if you prefer.

Ingredients:
1/2 whole skinless chicken breast

For the Marinade:
dash of salt
1 teaspoon rice wine or sherry
1 teaspoon cornstarch
4 dried black mushrooms*
1/4 cup dried golden lilies* (optional)
1/4 cup dried wood ears* (optional)
1/4 teaspoon black pepper
2 tablespoons vinegar (rice or white)
1 teaspoon sugar
2 tablespoons hot sauce
2 egg whites
4 cups chicken stock
1/4 cup julienned bamboo shoots*
4 oz. firm tofu, rinsed, drained and julienned
3 tablespoons cornstarch, dissolved in 1/2 cup water
2 green onions, chopped

available at Asian markets

Preparation:
Julienne chicken and marinate with salt, rice wine and cornstarch for 20 minutes. Soak dried black mushrooms, golden lilies and wood ears in hot water for 20 minutes; clean them and squeeze out excess water; cut ends off of mushrooms and lilies. Julienne mushrooms and wood ears. Lightly beat egg whites, set aside.

Directions:
In a nonstick pan with one spray of light vegetable oil, stir-fry chicken. When chicken separates and turns white, set aside.

Heat stock in a large saucepan on high heat. Stir in mushrooms, lilies, woodears, bamboo shoots, tofu and cooked chicken. Add pepper, vinegar, sugar and hot sauce. Bring to a boil, turn heat to low and simmer for 3 minutes. Stir in dissolved cornstarch and cook for another minute. Turn off the heat and add egg whites. Stir slowly with chopsticks in a clockwise direction for 20 seconds. Add chopped green onion garnish and serve.

Serves 6

Calories per serving: 113
Fat per serving: 2.1 grams
Calories from fat: 18%

Spinach Soup

*T*his soup looks as good as it tastes. Tofu is optional.

Ingredients:

1/2 (10 oz.) package frozen chopped spinach
4 cups stock (chicken or vegetable)
4 oz. soft tofu, cubed
3 tablespoons cornstarch dissolved in 1/4 cup water
dash of salt
2 egg whites

Preparation:

Defrost and squeeze out the excess water from frozen chopped spinach. Beat egg whites.

Directions:

In a medium saucepan, bring stock to a boil and add spinach, tofu and salt. Bring to a boil again. Stir in dissolved cornstarch and continue to cook, stir for 30 seconds. Turn off heat. Pour in egg whites and stir clockwise with chopsticks for 20 seconds.

Serves 4

*Calories per serving with
chicken stock: 81
Fat per serving with
chicken stock: 1 gram
Calories from fat: 12%*

*Calories per serving with
vegetable stock: 64
Fat per serving with
vegetable stock: 0.7 gram
Calories from fat: 10%*

Vegetable Stock

Y ou can use this basic and nutritious vegetable stock for
many recipes in this book which call for stock.

Ingredients:
6 dried black mushrooms*
8 cups water
6 green onions, cut in half
2 carrots, cut in half
4 celery stalks, cut in half
2 onions, cut into quarters
2 cloves garlic, mashed
6 slices fresh ginger
2 bay leaves
1/4 cup rice wine or dry sherry
dash of salt
dash of white pepper

*available at Asian markets

Preparation:
Soak black mushrooms in hot water for 20 minutes, clean,
drain and cut off the stems.

Directions:
In large saucepan, bring water to boil. Add green onions,
carrots, celery, onions, garlic, ginger, bay leaves, rice wine and
black mushrooms, reduce heat, simmer for 2 hours and add
salt and pepper. Remove vegetables (use a strainer if
necessary) from stock.

Stock can be frozen for one month for later use.

Makes 6 cups of stock

Calories per cup: 17
Fat per cup: trace
Calories from fat: 0%

Won Ton Soup

For won ton soup, you can use the same filling as in pot stickers, but use won ton skin wraps instead of pot sticker wraps, please see page 5. This soup can be served as a one-dish meal. Serve 15 won tons per person as a one-dish meal.

Ingredients:

6 cups water
20 uncooked, wrapped won tons
1 cup cold water
3 cups vegetable stock
1 tablespoon lite soy sauce
12 snow peas, deveined
6 baby corns from can, cut in half
1 green onion, chopped for garnish

Directions:

In a medium saucepan, bring 6 cups water to a boil, add won tons, stir occasionally to prevent sticking. Bring water to a boil and add one cup of cold water. Bring to boil again and drain won tons.

In the same saucepan, bring stock to a boil, add snow peas, baby corn and cook for 30 seconds. Add won tons back to pan and cook for another 20 seconds to bring the soup to a boil. Turn off the heat and garnish with green onions.

Serves 4

Calories per serving: 108
Fat per serving: 0.6 gram
Calories from fat: 5%

Main Courses

Ants Climbing a Tree

This is a well known dish from Szechwan. Ground turkey is used which resembles the ants; mung bean noodles resemble the branches of a tree. It is a great dish to serve with white rice.

Ingredients:
4 oz. dried mung bean noodles (also called bean thread cellophane noodles)*

For the Sauce:
2 cloves garlic, minced
2 tablespoons lite soy sauce
1 teaspoon rice wine or dry sherry
1 teaspoon hot sauce
1 teaspoon sugar

1 light vegetable oil spray
1/4 lb. ground turkey breast
1/2 cup chicken stock
2 green onions, chopped

available at Asian markets

Preparation:
Soak dried mung bean noodles in hot water for 15 minutes, drain and cut in thirds. Mix garlic, soy sauce, rice wine, hot sauce and sugar together; set aside.

Directions:

In a nonstick pan with one spray of light vegetable oil, stir-fry ground turkey and garlic. Separate ground turkey with a spatula while cooking until it is lightly browned. Add mung bean noodles and stock; cook for 1 minute. Add sauce, cook for another 2 minutes. Garnish with green onions before serving.

Serves 4

Calories per serving: 159
Fat per serving: 2 grams
Calories from fat: 12%

Boiled Crab with Dipping Sauce

Instead of high fat butter sauce, try the Chinese fat free version. Enjoy the full taste of crab. Fried rice may be an accompaniment later (see page 89).

Ingredients:
For the Dipping Sauce:
2 tablespoons lite soy sauce
2 tablespoons rice or white vinegar
2 tablespoons sugar
2 tablespoons minced fresh ginger

2 live crabs (use your favorite crab, dungeness or blue
   or 2 lbs. frozen crab legs)

8 cups water
3 green onions, cut in half
6 slices fresh ginger
1 (12 oz.) can of beer

Serves 2

Calories per serving: 181
Fat per serving: 0.6 gram
Calories from fat: 3%

Preparation:
Mix soy sauce, vinegar, sugar and ginger together for dipping sauce.

Directions:
Place crabs in a large saucepan, add water, green onion, ginger and beer. Bring to boil and cook for 15 minutes (if using frozen crab legs, cook 4 minutes longer). Drain, open shells and rinse with water. Crack shells, serve hot or chilled. Use sauce for dipping.

Chicken with Black Mushrooms

*T*his is my very best girlfriend's favorite dish. Add hot sauce for a spicier dish. Serve as a main course with a vegetable dish and rice.

Ingredients:
1 whole skinless chicken breast

For the Marinade:
dash of salt
1 tablespoon rice wine or dry sherry
1 tablespoon cornstarch
1 egg white

20 dried black mushrooms*
15 snow peas, deveined

1 light vegetable oil spray
2 tablespoons oyster sauce* (you may substitute soy sauce)
1 tablespoon hot sauce (optional)

available at Asian markets and some supermarkets

Preparation:
Cut chicken into strips about 2 x 1 inch pieces. Marinate with salt, rice wine, cornstarch and egg white for 20 minutes. Soak black mushrooms in hot water for 20 minutes. Clean, cut ends off and cut them in half; squeeze out any excess water.

Directions:

Spray a nonstick pan with 1 spray of light vegetable oil. Stir-fry chicken on high heat until chicken separates and turns white. Add black mushrooms, snow peas, oyster sauce and cook for 1 minute.

Add hot sauce to taste.

Serves 4

Calories per serving: 172
Fat per serving: 2 grams
Calories from fat: 11%

Chicken with Lima Beans

A wonderful combination of bean and chicken which has a delicate taste and is quite simple to prepare. Serve with rice as a main course.

Ingredients:
1/2 whole skinless chicken breast, cut in cubes

For the Marinade:
dash of salt
1 teaspoon rice wine or dry sherry
1 teaspoon cornstarch

2 cups frozen baby lima beans
1 light vegetable oil spray
2 garlic cloves, minced
1 cup chicken stock or water
dash of salt

1 teaspoon cornstarch dissolved in 3 tablespoons water
2 green onions, chopped

Preparation:
Marinate chicken with salt, rice wine and cornstarch for 20 minutes. Defrost lima beans.

Directions:

Spray a nonstick pan with 1 spray of light vegetable oil. Stir-fry chicken and garlic on high heat until chicken turns white and separates. Set aside.

In the same pan, cook lima beans in stock or water over medium high heat until they are tender. Add water if necessary. Return chicken back to the pan and add salt, dissolved cornstarch and green onion. Cook for an additional 30 seconds.

Serves 4

Calories per serving: 133
Fat per serving: 1.2 grams
Calories from fat: 9%

Chicken with Onions

I often had chicken with onion at lunch or dinner at home when I was a child. The Worcestershire sauce really gives a fabulous flavor. Serve with rice as a main course.

Ingredients:
1 whole skinless chicken breast

For the Marinade:
dash of salt
1 tablespoon rice wine or dry sherry
1 tablespoon cornstarch

1 light vegetable oil spray
2 tablespoons water
3 onions, thinly sliced

For the Sauce:
4 tablespoons Worcestershire sauce
1 tablespoon lite soy sauce
1/4 teaspoon black pepper
2 tablespoons sugar
2 tablespoons water

Preparation:

Cut chicken into 2 inch strips and marinate with salt, rice wine and cornstarch for 20 minutes. In separate bowl, mix together: Worcestershire sauce, soy sauce, black pepper, sugar and water.

Directions:

In a nonstick pan, coat pan with 1 spray of light vegetable oil. Stir-fry chicken until it separates and turns white. Set aside.

In the same pan, add 2 tablespoons water and stir-fry onion until lightly browned. Return cooked chicken to the pan and add prepared sauce. Cook for another 30 seconds.

Serves 4

Calories per serving: 166
Fat per serving: 1.9 grams
Calories from fat: 11%

Chicken with Peas

Y ou may substitute corn for peas if you prefer. It is a great dish served on rice as a whole meal.

Ingredients:
1 whole skinless chicken breast

For the Marinade:
dash of salt
1 tablespoon rice wine or sherry
1 tablespoon cornstarch

1 cup fresh or frozen peas
1 light vegetable oil spray
dash of salt

Serves 4

Calories per serving: 115
Fat per serving: 1.8 grams
Calories from fat: 15%

Preparation:
Cube chicken into 1/2 inch squares and marinate with salt, rice wine and cornstarch for 20 minutes. Wash peas and drain.

Directions:
Spray a nonstick pan with 1 spray of light vegetable oil. Stir-fry chicken till white and separated. Add peas, salt and cook for additional 30 seconds.

Chinese Green with Crab Meat

Y ou may use any leafy green vegetable for this dish. I prefer to use Chinese green such as bok choy which you may find in Asian markets or some supermarkets. Serve with any rice dish.

Ingredients:
1 lb. Chinese green
3 cups water
1 cup chicken stock or water
2 green onions, chopped
1 teaspoon minced fresh ginger

1 cup crab meat (fresh or frozen)

1 tablespoon rice wine or dry sherry
1 tablespoon oyster sauce*(can substitute soy sauce)
dash of salt
dash of white pepper

1 tablespoon cornstarch dissolved in 1/4 cup water

available at Asian markets

Preparation:
Clean greens and use only the tender parts.

Directions:
In a nonstick pan, boil 3 cups water and cook green vegetable for 4 minutes. Drain and arrange vegetable on a serving plate; keep warm.

In the same pan, boil 1 cup stock and add green onion, ginger and crab meat. Cook for 30 seconds on medium high heat, add wine, oyster sauce, salt and pepper and cook for an additional 30 seconds. Add dissolved cornstarch to thicken, cook 30 seconds more. Pour crab meat over vegetable to serve.

Serves 4

Calories per serving: 74
Fat per serving: 1 gram
Calories from fat: 13%

Freedom From Fat Chinese Home Cooking

Curry Chicken

Curry flavor can be made mild or hot to your taste. This is a wonderful one-dish meal served over white rice or brown rice. Top with a handful of raisins to add sweetness and texture.

Ingredients:
1 whole skinless chicken breast

For the Marinade:
dash of salt
1 tablespoon rice wine or dry sherry
1 tablespoon cornstarch

1 light vegetable oil spray
1/4 cup chicken stock or water
1 onion, 1 inch cubes
2 small carrots, 1 inch cubes
1 red potato, 1 inch cubes

For the Curry Sauce:
1 cup chicken stock
2 tablespoons sugar
3 tablespoons curry powder, or to taste
2 tablespoons cornstarch

1/2 cup evaporated skimmed milk, from can
1/4 cup raisins

Preparation:

Cut chicken into 1 inch cubes and marinate with salt, rice wine and cornstarch for 20 minutes. To make curry sauce, mix stock, sugar, curry powder and cornstarch together.

Directions:

In a nonstick pan, spray lightly with vegetable oil. Stir-fry chicken until it is white and begins to separate, set aside.

In the same pan, cook onion and stock until onion is lightly browned. Add carrots, potato and curry sauce. Bring mixture to a boil. Reduce to low heat and cover, simmer for 5 minutes or until carrots and potato are tender. Add evaporated skimmed milk and turn the heat off. Do not bring the mixture to a boil. Serve with a handful of raisins on top of rice.

Serves 6

Calories per serving: 171
Fat per serving: 1.9 grams
Calories from fat: 11%

Fish Fillet with Black Bean Sauce

Fermented black beans are used for seasoning in Southern Chinese cuisine. These beans can be found in Asian markets and are sold in small plastic bags. This is a great main dish to accompany any vegetable dish with steamed white rice.

Ingredients:
10 oz. fish fillet (cod or sea bass)

For the Marinade:
5 slices fresh ginger
dash of salt
1 tablespoon rice wine or dry sherry

For the Sauce:
2 tablespoons lite soy sauce
3 garlic cloves, minced
3 tablespoons fermented black beans,
   rinsed, drained and minced*
1/2 cup vegetable stock or water
1 tablespoon sugar
3 green onions, quartered

10 cilantro leaves

*available at Asian markets

Preparation:

Clean fillet and towel dry. Soak fillet in marinade on a plate, cover with plastic wrap. Mix soy sauce, garlic, black beans, stock, sugar and green onions together and heat in microwave for 2 minutes or cook on stove until boiling. Set aside.

Directions:

Place prepared fillet in microwave and cook for 3 minutes or steam for 8 minutes. Pour sauce on top and cover again, microwave for another 2 minutes or steam for another 3 minutes until fillet flakes with fork. Serve hot, garnished with fresh cilantro leaves.

Serves 6

Calories per serving
with cod: 69
Fat per serving
with cod: 0.4 gram
Calories from fat: 6%

Five Spiced Chicken

A terrific choice of spices put together make this dish unique. Add more hot sauce if you prefer spicy. Serve with rice as a main course.

Ingredients:
1 whole skinless chicken breast

For the Marinade:
dash of salt
1 tablespoon rice wine or dry sherry
1 tablespoon cornstarch

For the Sauce

1 tablespoon hot sauce
3 tablespoons sugar
4 teaspoons Worcestershire sauce
1 tablespoon water
1 teaspoon cornstarch

1 light vegetable oil spray
1 green onion, chopped
1 tablespoon minced fresh ginger
3 garlic cloves, minced
2 tablespoons chicken stock or water
10 water chestnuts, chopped
1 cup shredded lettuce

Preparation:

Julienne chicken and marinate with salt, rice wine and cornstarch for 20 minutes. In separate bowl mix together: hot sauce, sugar, Worcestershire sauce, water and dissolve cornstarch in this mixture.

Directions:

In a nonstick pan, spray 1 spray of light vegetable oil and stir-fry chicken on high heat until the chicken separates and turns white. Set aside.

In the same pan, add stock or water and water chestnuts and stir for 10 seconds over high heat. Add sauce, then return the chicken to the pan. Stir-fry for an additional 20 seconds. Serve hot on top of shredded lettuce.

Serves 4

Calories per serving: 212
Fat per serving: 2 grams
Calories from fat: 9%

Ground Turkey with Green Beans

 great dish to enjoy in all seasons. Omit turkey if you are vegetarian. Serve with rice.

Ingredients:
For the Sauce:

1 teaspoon hot sauce
1 tablespoon lite soy sauce
1 tablespoon sugar
1 teaspoon vinegar, rice or white
1 teaspoon cornstarch

2 cups water
1/2 lb. green beans, remove ends, cut in half
2 tablespoons water
1/4 lb. ground turkey breast
3 garlic cloves, minced
1 tablespoon chopped Chinese pickle* (optional)

*available at Asian markets

Preparation:
In a bowl mix together: hot sauce, soy sauce, sugar, vinegar and cornstarch. Set aside.

Directions:
In a nonstick pan, boil 2 cups water and cook green beans for 5 minutes. Drain and set aside.

In the same pan, add 2 tablespoons water and cook ground turkey, garlic and Chinese pickle. Stir-fry frequently until ground turkey is browned.

Return green beans to pan, cook with ground turkey and prepared sauce for 1 minute.

Serves 4

Calories per serving: 75
Fat per serving: 0.9 gram
Calories from fat: 12%

Hot Pot

This is my favorite dish for entertaining. Most Chinese dishes need to be cooked just before serving. This dish allows the host to enjoy the meal with her guests as well as the guests to enjoy cooking their own meal. Add any vegetable or seafood dish you wish. In the past, this was a traditional winter meal, but I serve it during all seasons. Serve with buns, Chinese pancakes, or fried rice.

Ingredients:

6 oz. mung bean noodles*(bean thread cellophane noodles)
1 whole skinless chicken breast, thinly sliced
8 oz. fillet (cod or sea bass), thinly sliced
1 pound or 20 large raw shrimp
20 snow peas, deveined
1 bunch fresh spinach, use leaves only
1/2 lb. Napa cabbage, cut into 2 inch pieces
4 oz. firm tofu

For the Sauce:

2 tablespoons oyster sauce
2 tablespoons lite soy sauce
1/4 teaspoon hot sauce
1 tablespoon sugar
1 tablespoon water
1 green onion, chopped
1 clove garlic, minced

For the Broth:

8 cups water
1/4 cup rice wine or dry sherry
2 green onions, cut in half

available at Asian markets

Hot Pot PAGE 45 and Steamed Buns PAGE 7

Preparation:

Soak mung bean noodles in hot water for 15 minutes, drain, cut in thirds. Arrange sliced chicken, fish fillet and shrimp on separate plates. Combine mung bean noodles and different vegetables on 2 large serving plates. Mix the dipping sauce together: oyster sauce, soy sauce, hot sauce, sugar, water, green onion and garlic. Set aside.

Directions:

Use a large electric frying pot or electric wok on the table with place settings for 6 people. Place uncooked dishes around pot. Fill pot with water, rice wine and green onions and bring it to a boil. Dip your choice of meats and vegetables into water, bring to a boil, let cook until done. Dip with sauce and repeat.

Serves 6

Calories per serving: 288
Fat per serving: 1.5 grams
Calories from fat: 5%

Calories per serving
with tofu: 298
Fat per serving
with tofu: 2.1 grams
Calories from fat: 7%

Freedom From Fat Chinese Home Cooking

Kung Pow Chicken

This is a well known dish that comes from the Province of Szechwan. By substituting water chestnuts for peanuts, you can reduce the fat content. Serve with rice as a main course.

Ingredients:
1 whole skinless chicken breast

For the Marinade:
dash of salt
1 tablespoon rice wine or dry sherry
1 teaspoon cornstarch

For the Sauce:
1/4 cup water
1 tablespoon hot sauce
2 tablespoons lite soy sauce
1 tablespoon rice wine or dry sherry
1 tablespoon vinegar, rice or white
2 tablespoons sugar
1 tablespoon cornstarch

1 light vegetable oil spray
3 cloves garlic, minced
10 water chestnuts, cubed*
12 dried red peppers, crushed.
1/4 cup water
2 green onions, chopped

*available at Asian markets and some supermarkets

Preparation:

Cut chicken in 1/2 inch cubes and marinate with salt, rice wine and cornstarch for 20 minutes. In separate bowl, mix together water, hot sauce, soy sauce, rice wine, vinegar, sugar and cornstarch.

Directions:

In a nonstick pan, with 1 spray of light vegetable oil, stir-fry marinated chicken and garlic till it separates and turns white, then add water chestnuts. Cook for 30 seconds and set aside.

In the same pan, stir-fry red peppers with 1/4 cup water for 30 seconds. Stir in chicken and water chestnuts, add prepared sauce and green onions. Stir-fry until sauce is well mixed and thickened with chicken and water chestnuts.

Serves 4

Calories per serving: 256
Fat per serving: 2.5 grams
Calories from fat: 10%

Lemon Chicken

This is a very popular dish with a great presentation. Without the traditional deep frying chicken and batter, we cut down the fat, but not the taste. Serve with rice as a main course.

Ingredients:
1 whole skinless chicken breast

For the Marinade:
dash of salt
1 tablespoon rice wine or dry sherry
1 tablespoon cornstarch

3 lemons
2 tablespoons lemon zest, from fresh lemon skin
5 slices fresh ginger
1/4 cup chicken stock or water
1/4 cup sugar
2 tablespoons cornstarch dissolved in 1/4 cup water

Preparation:

Cut chicken into 1 x 2 inch slices and marinate with salt, rice wine and cornstarch for 20 minutes. In a small bowl, peel lemon zest from lemons, cut lemons in half and squeeze out juice.

Directions:

In a nonstick pan with 1 spray of light vegetable oil, stir-fry chicken and ginger on high heat until chicken separates and turns white. Place chicken on a plate and set aside.

Add 1/4 cup stock or water to the same pan and heat on medium high, add lemon zest, lemon juice, sugar and stir until sugar is dissolved. Add dissolved cornstarch to thicken. Add chicken and stir for 30 seconds. Garnish with fresh lemon slices.

Serves 4

Calories per serving: 182
Fat per serving: 2.2 grams
Calories from fat: 12%

Mongolian Chicken

A great Northern dish which may be served on top of shredded lettuce as a main course. Serve with rice.

Ingredients:
1 whole skinless chicken breast

For the Marinade:
dash of salt
1 tablespoon rice wine or dry sherry
1 egg white
1 tablespoon cornstarch

For the Sauce:
1 tablespoon rice wine or dry sherry
1 teaspoon sugar
1 tablespoon lite soy sauce
2 tablespoons hoisin sauce*
2 tablespoons hot sauce or to your taste
1 teaspoon cornstarch

3 garlic cloves, minced
1 onion, thinly sliced
4 green onions, quartered

available at Asian markets

Preparation:
Slice chicken in 2 x 1 inch strips and marinate with salt, rice wine, egg white and cornstarch for 20 minutes. In separate bowl, mix together: rice wine, sugar, soy sauce, hoisin sauce, hot sauce and cornstarch. Set aside.

Directions:
In a nonstick pan, spray 1 spray of light vegetable oil and stir-fry chicken and garlic on high heat. When chicken begins to turn white and separate, add onion, green onions and stir-fry for 30 seconds. Add prepared sauce and cook for another 30 seconds.

Serves 4

Calories per serving: 114
Fat per serving: 1.7 grams
Calories from fat: 15%

Moo Shu Chicken

This dish will be a favorite among your guests. You can substitute homemade Chinese pancakes (see page 3) for fat free flour tortilla.

Ingredients:
1/2 whole skinless chicken breast
1/8 teaspoon salt
dash of black pepper
1 teaspoon rice wine or dry sherry
1 teaspoon cornstarch
6 dried black mushrooms
1/2 cup dried lilies* (optional)
1/4 cup dried wood ears* (optional)

1 light vegetable oil spray
3 cups julienned cabbage
1/2 cup julienned bamboo shoots*(optional)
2 tablespoons oyster sauce*(or substitute with soy sauce)
1 teaspoon cornstarch dissolved in 2 tablespoons water

3 green onion, quartered
1/4 cup hoisin sauce for serving*

*available at Asian markets

Preparation:
Julienne chicken and marinate for 20 minutes.

Soak black mushrooms in hot water for 10 minutes; clean and cut off the ends, squeeze out excess water and julienne. Soak lilies and wood ears in hot water for 20 minutes; clean and cut the hard ends off lilies, squeeze out the excess water and julienne wood ears.

Directions:
In a nonstick pan, use 1 spray of light cooking oil to stir-fry chicken until it is separated and turned white. Set aside.

In the same pan, use 1 spray of light cooking oil to stir-fry mushrooms, lilies, wood ears, cabbage, bamboo shoots in high heat for 1 minute. Return chicken to the pan and add oyster sauce, dissolved cornstarch, green onion then cook for another minute.

To Serve:
Spread 1 teaspoon hoisin sauce in the middle of pancake. Fill the pancake with 2 tablespoons of moo shu chicken, fold one end so the filling will not come out, then roll the pancake.

Serves 6

Calories per serving: 133
Fat per serving with pancake: 1.2 grams
Calories from fat: 14%

Red Sauce Fish

Red sauce can be used for cooking many different kinds of food such as fish, chicken, even vegetables. The basic ingredients for red sauce are soy sauce, rice wine, sugar and fresh ginger. The soy sauce gives a rich red color to the dish.

Ingredients:

1 light vegetable oil spray
12 oz. fresh fish fillet (cat fish, cod or sea bass)
3 cloves garlic, chopped
5 slices fresh ginger
2 green onions, quartered
1 tablespoon rice wine or dry sherry
3 tablespoons soy sauce
1 tablespoon sugar
1/2 cup chicken stock
1 green onion, chopped for garnish

Directions:

In a nonstick pan, spray once with light vegetable oil and brown fillet on both sides. Add garlic, ginger, green onions, rice wine, soy sauce, sugar and stock. Bring it to a boil and simmer covered for 5 minutes on low heat. Garnish with green onions.

Serves 4

Calories per serving: 112
Fat per serving: 1 gram
Calories from fat: 8%

Shrimp in Lobster Sauce

There is no lobster in this dish but it tastes like there is. Serve this with steamed white rice (see page 100).

Ingredients:
1 lb. or 20 large shrimp, shelled and deveined

For the Marinade:
1 tablespoon rice wine or dry sherry
dash of salt
1 egg white
1 tablespoon cornstarch
dash of white pepper

For the Sauce:
3 cloves garlic, chopped
1 tablespoon minced fresh ginger
2 green onions, chopped
1 tablespoon lite soy sauce
1 tablespoon rice wine or dry sherry
1 teaspoon sugar
dash of salt

2 egg whites
1/2 cup chicken stock or water
1/8 lb. ground turkey breast
1/4 cup green peas, fresh or frozen
2 tablespoons cornstarch dissolved in 1/4 cup water

Preparation:

Clean shrimp, towel dry and soak in marinade for 20 minutes. Prepare sauce. Beat egg whites, set aside.

Directions:

Pour 1/4 cup of stock in a nonstick pan and heat on high. Add shrimp, stirring until they are pink and firm. Remove shrimp from pan and set aside.

In the same pan, add remaining 1/4 cup stock and brown ground turkey on high heat. Add green peas, sauce, cook for 30 seconds. Return shrimp and add dissolved cornstarch to thicken. Turn heat off, slowly adding egg white with chopsticks stirring clockwise for 20 seconds.

Serves 4

Calories per serving: 184
Fat per serving: 1.8 grams
Calories from fat: 10%

Shrimp with Curry Sauce

$\mathbf{C}$urry adds great flavor to seafood. This dish can serve as a main dish and is best when accompanied by white or brown rice and vegetables.

Ingredients:
1 light vegetable oil spray
1 lb. or 20 large shrimp, shelled and deveined

For the Marinade:
1 egg white
1 tablespoon rice wine or dry sherry
dash of salt
dash of white pepper
1 tablespoon cornstarch

For the Curry Sauce:
3 tablespoons curry powder
1/2 cup chicken stock
1 tablespoon rice wine or dry sherry
1 tablespoon sugar
1 tablespoon cornstarch

1/4 cup canned evaporated skimmed milk
1 green onion, chopped

Preparations:

Marinate shrimp with egg white, rice wine, salt, pepper and cornstarch for 20 minutes in refrigerator. To make curry sauce, combine curry powder, stock, rice wine, sugar and cornstarch and mix until sauce is smooth.

Directions:

In a nonstick pan, spray 1 time with light vegetable oil spray and stir-fry shrimp until turned pink and firm. Add curry sauce and cook for 1 minute over medium heat. Add evaporated milk, green onion and turn the heat off. Do not let it come to a boil. Serve hot.

Serves 4

Calories per serving: 155
Fat per serving: 1 gram
Calories from fat: 6%

Shrimp with Peas

This is a mellow, soothing but tasty Shanghainess dish. Serve with any noodle or rice dish.

Ingredients:
20 large shrimp, shelled and deveined (about 1 lb. shrimp)

For the Marinade:
1 egg white
1 tablespoon rice wine or dry sherry
1 tablespoon cornstarch
dash of salt
dash of white pepper

1 light vegetable oil spray
4 slices fresh ginger
1 cup fresh or frozen peas
2 green onions, chopped
dash of salt

Serves 4

Calories per serving: 146
Fat per serving: 0.4 gram
Calories from fat: 3%

Preparation:
Clean shrimp with water, pat dry with paper towel. Add shrimp to marinade and chill for 20 minutes.

Directions:
Spray a nonstick pan with light vegetable oil, stir shrimp and ginger until shrimp is pink and firm. Add peas, green onion, salt and cook for 30 seconds.

Steamed Stuffed Cucumber

This dish is a beautiful jade color and the taste is fresh and delicate. Serve with steamed or fried rice.

Ingredients:
2 small regular cucumbers

For the Stuffing:
1/4 lb. ground turkey breast
1 egg white
1 teaspoon rice wine or dry sherry
2 green onions, chopped
1 tablespoon minced fresh ginger
dash of salt
dash of white pepper

For the Sauce:
1 tablespoon cornstarch
1 cup vegetable stock or water
dash of salt

Preparation:
Peel cucumbers, slice each cucumber into 8 pieces, or rings, remove seeds. In separate bowl, mix together: turkey, egg white, rice wine, green onions, ginger, salt and white pepper. Place stuffing inside each cucumber ring.

Directions:
Place cucumber rings on a plate and steam for 20 minutes. You can use a bamboo steamer as long as the pan fits into the steamer and it is possible to cover. Remove cucumber rings to a warm serving plate and arrange them evenly. Dissolve cornstarch in water, add salt, pour the remaining cucumber juice from the plate into this mixture and heat over high heat until mixture boils. To serve, pour sauce over cucumber rings.

Serves 4

Calories per serving: 76
Fat per serving: 1 gram
Calories from fat: 13%

Sweet and Sour Chicken

Not only will you fully enjoy the pungent mixture of sweet and sour flavors in this dish but, best of all, you won't miss the deep-fried chicken. Serve with rice as a main course.

Ingredients:
1 whole skinless chicken breast

For the Marinade:
dash of salt
1 tablespoon rice wine or dry sherry
1 tablespoon cornstarch
1 egg white

1 light vegetable oil spray

For the Sweet and Sour Sauce:
1/4 cup water
1/3 cup ketchup
1/2 cup sugar
2 tablespoons vinegar, rice or white
1 tablespoon cornstarch dissolved in 1/4 cup water

1/2 (8-oz.) can chunk pineapple, drained

Preparation:

Cut chicken in 2 x 1 inch strips and marinate in salt, rice wine, cornstarch and egg white for 20 minutes.

Directions:

In a nonstick pan, spray once with light vegetable oil and stir-fry chicken on high heat until chicken separates and turns white all the way through. Set aside.

In the same pan, boil 1/4 cup water, stir in ketchup, sugar and vinegar. Add dissolved corn starch to thicken the sauce. Return chicken to the pan and add the pineapple; cook for another 30 seconds.

Serves 4

Calories per serving: 243
Fat per serving: 4 grams
Calories from fat: 16%

Turkey Burger with Napa Cabbage

A family-style dish that is well loved by my family and friends. Serve with rice as a main course.

Ingredients:

For the Mixture:

1/2 lb. ground turkey breast
2 tablespoons lite soy sauce
2 tablespoons rice wine or dry sherry
2 egg whites
2 tablespoons minced fresh ginger
2 green onions, chopped
6 water chestnuts, chopped
1 teaspoon sugar
dash of salt
dash of black pepper
4 tablespoons all purpose flour

1 light vegetable oil spray
1 lb. Napa cabbage, sliced 1 x 2 inch pieces
3 tablespoons lite soy sauce
1 tablespoon sugar

Preparation:

In a large bowl, mix together: ground turkey, soy sauce, rice wine, egg whites, ginger, green onions, water chestnuts, sugar, salt, pepper and all purpose flour. Prepare 8 small patties.

Directions:

In a nonstick pan, spray 1 spray of light vegetable oil. Cook the patties 4 at a time, over medium high heat until they are brown on both sides; repeat with the remaining patties. Set aside.

In the same pan, cook Napa cabbage over high heat for 1 minute. Reduce heat to medium, add soy sauce and sugar and arrange the patties evenly on top of the Napa cabbage and simmer for 15 minutes before serving.

Serves 4

Calories per serving: 163
Fat per serving: 2.1 grams
Calories from fat: 12%

Freedom From Fat Chinese Home Cooking

Vegetables

Bell Peppers with Baked Bean Curd

Baked bean curd, made of soy beans, is sold in plastic bags in the refrigerated section of Asian markets and some supermarkets. Add hot sauce to the dish if you prefer spicy. Serve with steamed white rice.

Ingredients:

1 light vegetable oil spray
1 green bell pepper, seeded, julienned
1 red bell pepper, seeded, julienned
1 (10 oz.) package baked bean curd (soft), julienned*
3 cloves garlic, minced
1 tablespoon sugar
dash of salt
6 dried hot red peppers, mashed

available at Asian markets and some supermarkets

Directions:

In a nonstick pan with 1 spray of light vegetable oil, stir-fry bell peppers on high heat, add baked bean curd, garlic, cook for 1 minute.

Add sugar, salt and dried hot peppers, cook for another 30 seconds.

Serves 4

Calories per serving: 244
Fat per serving: 2.6 grams
Calories from fat: 11%

Black Beans with Bell Peppers PAGE 71

Black Beans with Bell Peppers

*T*his dish offers a beautiful color presentation and wonderful flavors. Serve this dish with white rice, or as an accompaniment to a main course.

Ingredients:

For the Sauce:

2 tablespoons fermented black beans*,
   rinsed, drained and minced
3 cloves garlic, minced
1 teaspoon sugar
2 tablespoons lite soy sauce
1/4 cup water
1 teaspoon cornstarch

2 tablespoons water
1 onion, sliced
1 red pepper, cut in half, seeded and sliced
   into 1 x 2 inch pieces
1 green pepper, cut in half, seeded and sliced
   into 1 x 2 inch pieces
1 yellow pepper, cut in half, seeded and sliced
   into 1 x 2 inch pieces

available at Asian markets

Preparation:

Mix black bean, garlic, sugar, soy sauce, water and cornstarch together, set aside.

Directions:

In a nonstick pan, add 2 tablespoons water and onion, stir-fry on high heat until lightly browned. Add peppers and stir-fry for 1 minute, stir in sauce and mix well.

Serves 4

Calories per serving: 204
Fat per serving: 1.7 grams
Calories from fat: 8%

Freedom From Fat Chinese Home Cooking

Broccoli, Cauliflower and Baby Corn

This is a beautiful complement to any main dish. Serve with rice.

Ingredients:

2 cups broccoli florets
2 cups cauliflower florets
1/2 (15-oz.) can young corn, drained*

For the Sauce:

1 cup vegetable stock or water
2 garlic cloves, minced
1 teaspoon minced fresh ginger
2 tablespoons oyster sauce* (can substitute soy sauce)
1 tablespoon rice wine or dry sherry
pinch of white pepper
1 tablespoon cornstarch dissolved in 1/4 cup water

available at Asian markets

Directions:

Steam broccoli and cauliflower florets for 5 minutes in a bamboo steamer or a regular steamer. Add young corn to steam another 5 minutes, arrange vegetables in 3 groups on a serving plate and keep warm; set aside.

In a small saucepan, bring stock to a boil, add garlic, ginger, oyster sauce, rice wine, pepper and bring to a boil again. Stir in dissolved cornstarch to thicken. Pour sauce over arranged vegetables and serve hot.

Serves 4

Calories per serving: 119
Fat per serving: 1 gram
Calories from fat: 8%

Cauliflower and Peas

A great Shanghainess vegetarian dish to accompany a main dish. Instead of peas, you may substitute fresh mushrooms or dried black mushrooms.

Ingredients:

3 cups cauliflower florets
5 slices fresh ginger
1/4 cup vegetable stock or water
1 cup fresh or frozen peas
dash of salt
1 teaspoon sugar
1 teaspoon cornstarch dissolved in 3 tablespoons water

Serves 4

Calories per serving: 68
Fat per serving: 0.6 gram
Calories from fat: 9%

Directions:

In a nonstick pan, stir-fry cauliflower with ginger slices in water over high heat for 1 minute. Add peas, salt and sugar. Reduce heat to medium high and cook for an additional minute, or until cauliflower is soft. Add dissolved cornstarch to thicken.

Egg Fu Yong

By pan frying egg fu yong instead of deep frying, you will not sacrifice any flavor or texture. Serve as a main or side dish with rice.

Ingredients:

For the Sauce:

1/2 cup chicken stock
2 tablespoons oyster sauce*(can substitute soy sauce)
dash of white pepper
1 tablespoon cornstarch dissolved in 1/4 cup water

1/4 lb. fresh bean sprouts
2 green onions, chopped
1 light vegetable oil spray
1 cup egg substitute

*available at Asian markets

Serves 6

Calories per serving: 57
Fat per serving: 1 gram
Calories from fat: 17%

Preparation:

To make sauce: in a nonstick pan, bring stock to boil, add oyster sauce, dash of white pepper and dissolved cornstarch, keep warm and set aside. Mix bean sprouts and green onions together.

Directions:

Use the same pan after cleaning, spray 1 time with light vegetable oil. On medium high heat, add 1 pile of bean sprouts (about 1/4 cup) and green onions, cook for 10 seconds. Pour 3 tablespoons egg substitute over bean sprouts and green onion. Cook until firm and flip over. Repeat if needed until both sides are browned. Set on a large serving plate and repeat with remaining sprouts. Arrange egg fu yong evenly on a serving plate, pour sauce over before serving.

Five Spice Eggplant

C hinese eggplants are shaped like bananas but have smaller seeds. They are available at Asian markets and some supermarkets. Add hot sauce to your own taste. Can be served with rice or as a side dish to a main course.

Ingredients:

For the Sauce:

2 tablespoons lite soy sauce
1 tablespoon vinegar (rice or white)
3 tablespoons sugar
1 tablespoon hot sauce
1 teaspoon cornstarch
1 light vegetable oil spray

1 lb. eggplant (prefer Chinese eggplant)*,
   cut in half and in 1 1/2 inch slices, do not peel
4 slices fresh ginger
1 cup water

available at Asian markets and some supermarkets

Preparation:

Mix soy sauce, vinegar, sugar, hot sauce and cornstarch together.

Directions:

In a nonstick pan with 1 spray of light vegetable oil, stir eggplant and ginger over high heat. Add water and cook for 2 minutes or until eggplant is soft. If eggplant is dry, add more water. Add sauce and cook for one more minute.

Serves 4

Calories per serving: 77
Fat per serving: 0.5 gram
Calories from fat: 6%

Freedom From Fat Chinese Home Cooking

Garlic Vegetable

This is a colorful dish that can be served with rice or accompany a main course.

Ingredients:

1/4 cup vegetable stock or water
4 garlic cloves, minced
1 small carrot, julienned
1 small zucchini, julienned
1/4 lb. bean sprouts
3 green onions, quartered
dash of salt

Directions:

In a nonstick pan, add water, garlic and carrot, bring to boil on high heat. Add zucchini, cook for 30 seconds. Add bean sprouts and green onions, cook for another 30 seconds. Add salt before serving.

Serves 4

Calories per serving: 25
Fat per serving: 0.2 gram
Calories from fat: 8%

Lettuce with Oyster Sauce

This is a simple, but all-purpose, side dish for main courses.

Ingredients:
5 cups water
1/2 head lettuce (prefer iceberg)
3 tablespoons oyster sauce*

*available at Asian markets

Directions:
In a large saucepan, bring water to boil over high heat. Add lettuce and cook for 1 minute. Remove lettuce and drain. Arrange lettuce evenly on a large plate and top with oyster sauce.

Serves 4

Calories per serving: 18
Fat per serving: 0.2 gram
Calories from fat: 11%

Freedom From Fat Chinese Home Cooking

Ma Pou Tofu

ofu is also known as bean curd which is made from fresh soy beans. This is a family-style dish that is served with white rice. If you wish, add hot sauce to your taste.

Ingredients:

For the Sauce:

3 tablespoons water
3 tablespoons oyster sauce*(can substitute soy sauce)
1 tablespoon rice wine or dry sherry
1 tablespoon cornstarch

1 light vegetable oil spray
3 cloves garlic, minced
2 cups sliced fresh mushrooms
8 oz. firm tofu, drained, cubed
2 green onions, chopped

*available at Asian markets

Serves 4

Calories per serving: 70
Fat per serving: 1.6 grams
Calories from fat: 22%

Preparation:

Mix water, oyster sauce, rice wine and cornstarch together as sauce, set aside.

Directions:

Spray a nonstick pan with 1 spray of light vegetable oil, add garlic and mushrooms and cook on high heat for 30 seconds. Add tofu, sauce I and cook for 1 minute. Add green onion before serving.

Moo Shu Vegetables

Moo shu vegetables is a Northern Chinese classic. Your guests will enjoy rolling their own Chinese pancakes (see page 3) with moo shu vegetables. You can also substitute egg for chicken if you prefer.

Ingredients:

6 dried black mushrooms*
1/2 cup dried lilies*(optional)
1/4 cup dried wood ears*(optional)
1 light vegetable oil spray
4 oz. egg substitute or 6 egg whites
3 cups julienned cabbage
1/2 cup julienned bamboo shoots*(optional)
2 tablespoons oyster sauce*(can substitute soy sauce)
1 teaspoon cornstarch dissolved in 2 tablespoons water
3 green onions, quartered
1/4 cup hoisin sauce for serving*

available at Asian markets

Preparation:

Soak black mushrooms in hot water for 10 minutes; clean and cut off the ends, squeeze out excess water and julienne. Soak lilies and wood ears in hot water for 20 minutes; clean and cut the hard ends off lilies, squeeze out the excess water and julienne wood ears.

Directions:
In a nonstick pan, use 2 sprays of light cooking oil to scramble egg substitute or egg whites. Set aside.

In the same pan, use 1 spray of light cooking oil to stir-fry mushrooms, lilies, wood ears, cabbage and bamboo shoots on high heat for 1 minute. Return eggs to the pan. Add oyster sauce, dissolved cornstarch and green onion and cook for another minute.

To Serve:
Spread 1 teaspoon hoisin sauce in the middle of a pancake. Fill the pancake with 2 tablespoons of moo shu vegetables, fold one end so the filling will not come out, then roll the pancakes.

Serves 6

Calories per serving with pancake: 106
Fat per serving with pancake: 1.2 grams
Calories from fat: 11%

Mushrooms

This dish calls for dry or fresh black shiitake mushrooms. Traditionally, dry mushrooms are used but they must be soaked in hot water for 20 minutes. Serve this dish with rice as a side dish.

Ingredients:

20 dried black mushrooms*
1/2 lb. fresh mushrooms
1/2 cup vegetable stock
2 garlic cloves, minced
2 tablespoons oyster sauce*(can substitute soy sauce)
1 tablespoon cornstarch dissolved in 1/4 cup water

available at Asian markets and some supermarkets

Preparation:

Soak black mushrooms in hot water for 20 minutes. Clean, squeeze excess water out and cut ends off. Clean fresh mushrooms; cut ends off and slice each mushroom in 4 slices.

Directions:

In a nonstick pan, add stock and garlic; bring to a boil. Add black mushrooms. Reduce heat to medium and cook for 2 minutes. Add fresh mushrooms and cook for 30 seconds. Add oyster sauce and dissolved cornstarch. If it is dry, add 2 tablespoons water.

Serves 4

Calories per serving: 94
Fat per serving: 0.5 gram
Calories from fat: 5%

Spicy Cucumber Salad

Y ou won't miss the fat in this spicy treat! It is perfect with a main course or noodle dish.

Ingredients:
2 cucumbers

For the Sauce:
3 dried hot red peppers, crushed
1/4 cup vinegar (rice or white)
2 tablespoons sugar
dash of salt
1 teaspoon lite soy sauce
2 green onions, chopped
1/4 cup chopped fresh cilantro

Preparation:
Peel the cucumbers, cut in half lengthwise. Clean seeds out with a small spoon and slice in small pieces. In a small bowl, mix crushed hot peppers, vinegar, sugar, salt and soy sauce. Microwave for 1 minute, or heat on stove till sugar is dissolved, let cool and set aside.

Directions:
In a large bowl, combine cucumbers and sauce, mix well and leave in refrigerator for 30 minutes or longer. Add green onion, cilantro and toss well before serving.

Serves 4

Calories per serving: 60
Fat per serving: 0.3 gram
Calories from fat: 5%

Steamed Eggplant

I recommend this light, summery eggplant dish served with rice or as a complement to a main course.

Ingredients:

1 lb. eggplant, preferably Chinese (about 2 Chinese eggplants), do not peel*.

For the Sauce:

2 garlic cloves, minced
1 teaspoon minced ginger
2 tablespoons lite soy sauce
2 tablespoons sugar
1 tablespoon hot sauce

*available at Asian markets

Serves 4

Calories per serving: 63
Fat per serving: 0.2 gram
Calories from fat: 3%

Preparation:

Cut eggplant in half and quarter each half. Place eggplant on a plate and set aside. Mix garlic, ginger, soy sauce, sugar and hot sauce in a medium bowl and microwave for 2 minutes or heat on stove till sugar is dissolved. Set aside.

Directions:

Place eggplant in a steamer and steam for 20 minutes or until tender. When eggplant is cool, shred with hands and place on a serving plate. Pour sauce over eggplant and serve hot or cold.

Tomato and Soy Bean Sprouts

Soy bean sprouts come from soy beans unlike bean sprouts which come from mung beans. This is a pretty and nutritious vegetable dish that will complement any main course. Serve with rice.

Ingredients:

1/2 lb. fresh soy bean sprouts*
1 light vegetable oil spray
2 tomatoes, cut in quarters
2 tablespoons water
dash of salt
1 tablespoon sugar

*available at Asian markets

Preparation:

Clean, pick out bad soy bean sprouts; drain well.

Directions:

Lightly spray a nonstick pan, then stir-fry tomatoes over high heat for 1 minute. Add water and cook until tomatoes are very soft. Add soy bean sprouts and cook for another minute, add salt and sugar.

Serves 4

Calories per serving: 66
Fat per serving: 2.5 grams
Calories from fat: 4%

Rice & Noodles

Brown Rice

Brown rice is nutritious and has a wonderful texture. It can be prepared in advance and reheated before serving.

Ingredients:
1 cup brown rice
2 cups water

Preparation:
Rinse rice with cold water, drain. Repeat.

Directions:
In a medium saucepan, bring rice and 2 cups water to boil. Reduce heat to low, cover, simmer for 40 minutes or until rice is tender and water is absorbed. Fluff rice with fork before serving.

Makes 3 cups brown rice.

Serves 4

Calories per serving: 170
Fat per serving: 1 gram
Calories from fat: 6%

Cold Noodle from Szechwan

This dish, also called "Tan-tan-min," is very spicy. The Szechwan and Hunan provinces are home to the spiciest and most fiery Chinese cuisines.

Ingredients:

1 tablespoon peppercorns*

For the Sauce:

1/4 cup chicken stock
1/4 cup lite soy sauce
2 tablespoons hot sauce
1 tablespoon vinegar (rice or white)
2 cloves garlic, minced
1 teaspoon minced fresh ginger
1 tablespoon sugar

2 cups water
1 whole skinless chicken breast
8 cups water
1/2 lb. linguine
1/2 cup chicken stock
2 cups shredded lettuce
1/2 cup bean sprouts (washed and drained)
1/2 cup chopped water chestnuts**
3 chopped green onions

*available at Asian markets
**available at Asian markets and some supermarkets

Preparation:

To make sauce, toast peppercorns in small toaster oven or regular oven at 450 degrees for 2 minutes. Crush them in medium bowl, add stock, soy sauce, hot sauce, vinegar, garlic, ginger and sugar; mix well. Place bowl in microwave for 2 minutes or heat on stove till boiling. Set aside.

In a medium saucepan, add 2 cups water and cook chicken for 5 minutes on medium high heat or until chicken is white inside and out. Chill chicken and shred, set aside.

In a large saucepan, boil 8 cups of water and cook linguine until *al dente*. Rinse with cold water and drain. Place linguine in a large bowl, add 1/2 cup stock and toss well.

To Serve:

On a large serving plate, spread lettuce out evenly as the first layer, add bean sprouts as second, linguine as third, chicken as fourth and top with water chestnuts and green onion. Pour sauce over before serving.

Serves 4

Calories per serving: 332
Fat per serving: 2.8 grams
Calories from fat: 8%

"Fried Rice"

Leftover rice is the best base material for fried rice. Add other ingredients such as: chicken, shrimp, black mushrooms, fresh mushrooms, or other vegetables. Serve as a main course and accompany with a soup, or as a side dish with a main course.

Ingredients:
1 light vegetable oil spray
8 oz. egg substitute
1/4 cup water
2 onions, chopped
1/4 cup chopped celery
1/2 cup fresh or frozen peas
2 cups cooked rice
3 tablespoon oyster sauce* (soy sauce may be substituted)
dash of white pepper
2 green onions, chopped for garnish

available at Asian markets

Directions:
Spray a nonstick pan with 1 spray of the light vegetable oil and heat at a high setting. Stir-fry egg substitute until it is well scrambled. Break mixture apart into small pieces with a spatula. Set aside.

Heat pan on high again with 1/4 cup water. Stir in onions and cook for 2 minutes, or until lightly browned. Add celery and peas, stir-fry for 1 minute, then set aside.

Heat the pan a final time with 1 spray of the light vegetable oil. Using your hands, break rice apart into the pan. Stir-fry rice for 1 minute, then add oyster sauce. Cook rice thoroughly, add onion, celery, peas and egg substitute. Reduce the heat; add pepper and green onion before serving.

Serves 6

Calories per serving: 161
Fat per serving: 1.8 grams
Calories from fat: 11%

Northern Sauce Noodle

This is a flavorful one-dish meal that works well in all seasons.

Ingredients:
For the Sauce:
1 1/2 cups chicken stock
1/2 tablespoon bean paste* or lite soy sauce
1 tablespoon sugar
1 tablespoon hot sauce
1 tablespoon rice wine or dry sherry

1 light vegetable oil spray
2 onions, cubed
1/2 lb. ground turkey breast
1/4 cup cornstarch dissolved in 1/2 cup water
8 cups water
1/2 lb. linguine
1/2 cup chicken stock
1 cup shredded lettuce

available at Asian markets

Preparation:
In a bowl, mix sauce together: stock, bean paste, sugar, hot sauce and rice wine. Set aside.

Directions:
Spray a nonstick pan with 1 spray of light vegetable oil. Stir-fry onions and ground turkey on high heat until they are lightly browned. Add prepared sauce and cook for 1 minute. Add dissolved cornstarch to thicken. Set aside.

In a large saucepan, bring 8 cups water to boil, cook linguine until *al dente*. Drain linguine, toss with 1/2 cup stock and divide into 4 large serving bowls. Top with shredded lettuce and turkey sauce.

Serves 4

Calories per serving: 418
Fat per serving: 5 grams
Calories from fat: 12%

Shanghainess Noodle

I grew up having this noodle dish for lunch. The Chinese pickled cabbage made this dish different from others. It can be found in small cans in Asian markets.

Ingredients:
1/2 whole skinless chicken breast

For the Marinade:
dash of salt
1 teaspoon rice wine or dry sherry
1 teaspoon cornstarch

2 cups chicken stock
1 light vegetable oil spray
1 tablespoon minced fresh ginger
2 cups julienned bamboo shoots*
1 (7 oz.) can chopped Chinese pickled cabbage, drained**
8 cups water
1/2 lb. linguine

*available at Asian markets and some supermarkets
**available at Asian markets

Preparation:
Julienne chicken and marinate with salt, rice wine and cornstarch for 20 minutes. Keep 2 cups of stock hot for serving.

Directions:

Spray a nonstick pan with 1 spray of light vegetable oil. Stir-fry chicken over high heat until it is white and begins to separate. Add ginger, bamboo shoots, Chinese pickled cabbage and cook for 1 minute. Set aside.

In a large saucepan, bring 8 cups water to boil and cook linguine until *al dente*. Drain well and divide into four large serving bowls. Add 1/2 cup stock to each bowl, topping with chicken, bamboo shoots and Chinese pickled cabbage.

Serves 4

Calories per serving: 325
Fat per serving: 2.4 grams
Calories from fat: 7%

Stir-Fry Rice Cakes

$\mathbf{R}$ ice cakes are made from white rice and are usually sold pre-sliced in the frozen food section of Asian markets. They can be served for breakfast, dim-sum or dinner.

Ingredients:
1 (16 oz.) package frozen or fresh sliced rice cake*
1/2 whole skinless chicken breast

For the Marinade:
dash of salt
1 teaspoon rice wine or dry sherry
1 teaspoon cornstarch

1 tablespoon minced fresh ginger
1 cup julienned bamboo shoots*
1 (7 oz.) can chopped pickled cabbage, drained*

available at Asian markets

Preparation:
Soak rice cakes in water overnight and drain. Julienne chicken and marinate with salt, rice wine and cornstarch for 20 minutes.

Directions:

In a nonstick pan with 1 spray of light vegetable oil, stir-fry chicken and ginger over high heat. When the chicken is separated and has turned white, add bamboo shoots, pickled cabbage and cook for 30 seconds, set aside.

In the same pan, spray 3 times with light vegetable oil and cook rice cakes over medium high heat for 1 minute or until they are soft. Return chicken, bamboo shoots and pickled cabbage to the pan and cook for an additional 30 seconds.

Serves 6

Calories per serving: 386
Fat per serving: 2.9 grams
Calories from fat: 8%

Vegetable Lo Mein

This is a light version of a classic noodle dish. The fresh Chinese noodles can be found in the refrigerated foods section in Asian markets. Serve casually as a one-dish meal or as a side dish with main courses.

Ingredients:

For the Noodle:

6 cups water
10 oz. fresh Chinese noodles* (can substitute fresh pasta such as linguine)
1/4 cup vegetable stock

1 light vegetable oil spray
3 leeks, white part only, cut into thin slices
2 cloves garlic, minced
1/2 lb. bok choy, cut into 1 1/2 inch pieces
20 snow peas, deveined
1/4 (15-oz.) can young corn, drained, cut into 1 inch pieces*
1/4 lb. bean sprouts
3/4 cup vegetable stock
2 tablespoons oyster sauce* (can substitute soy sauce)
dash of salt
dash of white pepper
1 tablespoon cornstarch dissolved in 1/4 cup water

available at Asian markets

Directions:

In a medium saucepan, bring water to boil, cook noodles for 4 minutes or until *al dente*. Rinse with cold water, drain and toss with 1/4 cup stock, set aside.

In a nonstick pan, spray one time with light vegetable oil, stir-fry leek and garlic for 30 seconds, add bok choy, snow peas, young corn, bean sprouts and cook for another 30 seconds. Add 3/4 cup stock, oyster sauce, salt, pepper and dissolved cornstarch. Add noodles and mix, toss well together, serve hot.

Serves 6

Calories per serving: 181
Fat per serving: 2 grams
Calories from fat: 11%

Vegetable Rice

$\top$his is a nostalgic one-dish meal that also can be served with soup.

Ingredients:
10 dried black mushrooms*
1 light vegetable oil spray
3/4 lb. bok choy, cut in 1 inch pieces
1 tablespoon rice wine or dry sherry
dash of salt
dash of sugar
2 cups white rice
1 cup water
2 cups vegetable stock

available at Asian markets

Preparation:
Soak black mushrooms in hot water for 15 minutes, clean, cut off ends, squeeze excess water out and slice into small strips.

Directions:
In a nonstick pan, spray once with vegetable oil spray, stir-fry black mushrooms and bok choy for 1 minute. Add rice wine, salt and sugar, cook for another 30 seconds, set aside.

In a medium saucepan, wash rice and drain. Add water and stock and bring to a boil, stirring occasionally. Leave uncovered until all liquid is almost absorbed. Add cooked black mushrooms and bok choy, mix well. Reduce heat to low and simmer, covered, for 20 minutes or until rice is tender. Turn heat off and let rice sit for 10 minutes. Fluff rice with fork before serving.

Serves 6

Calories per serving: 129
Fat per serving: 0.6 gram
Calories from fat: 5%

White Rice

White rice is the basic food in Chinese cuisine. It is served with all dishes and soups. It also can be prepared in advance and reheated before serving.

Ingredients:
1 cup white rice
1 1/2 cups water

Preparation:
Rinse rice with cold water, drain. Repeat until water is clear.

Directions:
In a medium saucepan, bring rice and 1 1/2 cups water to boil, uncovered, until water is almost absorbed. Reduce heat to low and simmer, covered, for 15 minutes or until rice is tender. Fluff rice with fork before serving.

Makes 3 cups white rice

Serves 4

Calories per serving: 145
Fat per serving: 0.6 gram
Calories from fat: 4%

Desserts

Almond Chocolate Cookies

$\mathcal{T}$he flavor of almonds is revered by the Chinese. These cookies are light and delicious. Serve as dessert or snack.

Ingredients:
2 large egg whites
6 tablespoons sugar
1 tablespoon cocoa powder
1/2 teaspoon almond extract

Directions:
Preheat oven to 300˚. Beat egg whites until stiff enough to hold soft peaks. While beating, slowly add the sugar, cocoa powder and almond extract.

Use a tablespoon to drop the cookie mixture onto a nonstick cookie sheet. Bake for 20 minutes.

Makes about 20 cookies

Calories per cookie: 21
Fat per cookie: 0.2 gram
Calories from fat: 9%

Corn Pancakes

These can be served at breakfast or afternoon dim-sum. Serve plain or with honey or syrup.

Ingredients:
4 egg whites
1/2 cup all purpose flour
1/4 cup sugar
1 teaspoon baking powder
1/2 (15 oz.) can cream-style corn

1 light vegetable oil spray

Makes about 12 pancakes

Calories per pancake: 54
Fat per pancake: 0.2 gram
Calories from fat: 4%

Preparation:
Beat egg whites until fluffy; set aside.

Directions:
Mix flour, sugar and baking powder; add cream-style corn and mix well. Slowly fold in egg whites.

Over medium high heat, spray a nonstick pan one time with the light vegetable oil. Pour 4 tablespoons of pancake mixture into the heated pan. Cook until lightly brown on both sides. Repeat the rest.

Freedom From Fat Chinese Home Cooking

Mung Beans and Barley Soup

The Chinese like to serve soup before a main course and serve sweet soup after a main course as a dessert or for breakfast. This soup can be served chilled in the summer or served warm in the winter.

Ingredients:
1/2 cup mung beans*
1/4 cup pearl barley
9 cups water
1 cup sugar

*available at Asian markets

Directions:
Rinse beans and pearl barley, remove bad beans.

In a medium saucepan, bring beans, barley and 6 cups water to a boil. Cook beans and barley over high heat for 50 minutes, uncovered. Stirring occasionally, add remaining 3 cups water, add sugar, turn off heat and let sit for 15 minutes before chilling in refrigerator or serving warm.

Serves 6

Calories per serving: 218
Fat per serving: 0.3 gram
Calories from fat: 1%

Red Bean Soup

This is another sweet soup serving as a dessert. Red bean soup is nutritious and delicious. The Chinese believe that during cold weather this soup warms the heart.

Ingredients:

3/4 cup dried Chinese red beans*
20 dried Chinese red dates* (jujubes)
9 cups water
3/4 cup brown sugar

*available at Asian markets

Serves 6

Calories per serving: 238
Fat per serving: 0.4 gram
Calories from fat: 1%

Directions:

Rinse beans, remove bad beans. If possible, allow beans to soak overnight to cut down the cooking process.

In a medium saucepan, cook beans and 7 cups water over a high heat, uncovered, for 1 hour, stirring occasionally. Add dates and remaining 2 cups water and cook for another hour on medium heat until beans are very soft and partially opened. Add sugar to serve.

Steamed Angel Cake PAGE 107

Steamed Angel Cake

This is a light, fresh and wonderful dessert which can be served with fresh strawberries and strawberry sauce, peach topping, non-fat yogurt, other fresh fruit or just plain. Serve hot or cool.

Ingredients:

10 egg whites
1 light vegetable oil spray
1 cup all-purpose flour
1 cup sugar
1 tablespoon baking powder
1/4 cup water

For the Strawberries and Strawberry Sauce:

1 cup fresh sliced strawberries
1/2 cup sugar
1/2 cup fresh sliced strawberries

For the Peach Topping:

2 fresh peaches
1/2 cup sugar

Preparation:

Beat 5 egg whites until stiff. Set aside. Spray a 9 inch bundt pan with light vegetable oil. Set aside.

Directions:

Mix flour, sugar and baking powder in a large bowl. Slowly add water and the remaining 5 egg whites. Mix thoroughly. Fold in the beaten egg whites. Pour the mixture into prepared bundt pan. You can use a bamboo steamer as long as pan fits into the steamer and it is possible to cover. Steam for 30 minutes, covered, on high heat. The cake is done when a wooden pick inserted into the center comes out clean.

Fresh Strawberries and Strawberry Topping:

Blend 1 cup strawberries and sugar till liquid. For serving, pour sauce over each slice of cake and garnish with fresh sliced strawberries.

Peach Topping:

Peel and slice peaches. Place slices in a bowl, add sugar, mix well. Let it set for 10 minutes before pouring over each slice of cake before serving.

Serves 8

Calories per cake serving: 177
Fat per cake serving: 0.3 gram
Calories from fat: 1%

Calories per strawberries and strawberry sauce serving: 57
Fat per strawberries and strawberry sauce serving: 0.1 gram
Calories from fat: 2%

Calories per peach topping serving: 58
Fat per peach topping serving: 0.02 gram
Calories from fat: trace

Steamed Pears

*T*he Chinese often serve fruit as dessert. This is a dessert I often had when I was in Shanghai.

Ingredients:
4 pears
4 tablespoons honey or brown sugar, or Chinese rock sugar*
4 fresh strawberries, sliced
2 fresh kiwis, peeled, sliced

available at Asian markets

Serves 4

Calories per serving: 160
Fat per serving: 0.9 gram
Calories from fat: 5%

Directions:
Slice off each tip of unpeeled pear (about 1 1/2 inch from the tip) to use as a lid. Core each pear and add 1 tablespoon honey inside of each pear and put the tip of pear back. Insert 2 wooden sticks on both sides of each pear lid to secure the closure while steaming. Use regular or bamboo steamer to steam pears for 30 minutes or until pears are tender. You may microwave pears for 5 minutes or until they are tender. Serve hot, garnish with colorful fresh fruit such as slices of fresh strawberries and slices of kiwis.

Tofu-less Almond Tofu

This refreshingly sweet and light traditional dessert resembles tofu in color and consistency.

Ingredients:

1 1/2 cups water
2 envelopes Knox unflavored gelatin or 2 tablespoons agar-agar
1/2 cup sugar
1 cup nonfat milk
1 teaspoon almond extract
1 1/4 cups water
1/2 cup sugar
1 (1 lb. 4 oz.) can litchi or other canned fruit
1 (11 oz.) can mandarin oranges

Directions:

Bring 1 1/2 cups of water to a boil in a medium saucepan. Stir in gelatin until completely dissolved. Remove from heat. Add sugar, milk, almond extract and mix well until sugar is dissolved. Pour into an 8 x 8 inch pan or dish, refrigerate for 2 hours or until firm. Cut in cubes and place in a large serving bowl.

Bring 1 1/4 cups water to boil in a small saucepan, stir in 1/2 cup sugar until dissolved. Cool completely and pour over cubes. Add litchi or other fruit and mandarin oranges to serving bowl. Refrigerate 30 minutes before serving.

Serves 6

Calories per serving: 247
Fat per serving: 0.6 gram
Calories from fat: 2%

Index

A

B

C

Fish:
   Fish Fillet with Black Bean Sauce, 40
   Hot Pot, 45
   Red Sauce Fish, 56
Five Spiced Chicken, 42
Five Spice Eggplant, 75
Fried:
   "Fried Rice," 89
   Stir-Fried Rice Cakes, 95
   "Un-Fried" Crab Cakes, 12
   "Un-Fried" Egg Rolls, 13

Garlic Vegetable, 76
Ground Turkey with Green Beans, 44

Hot and Sour Soup, 19
Hot Pot, 45

K

Kung Pow Chicken, 48

L

Lemon Chicken, 50
Lettuce with Oyster Sauce, 77

M

N

V

W